HOW TO BE FRANK
WITH YOUR FRIENDS

STAGE

ho
ho
ho

LA
20 Cigarros Finos
MATADoRA
establecido 1881
Hecho en La Habana
Maduro

Barber
Shop

Glass Slipper

No Peeking!

SEMENT

PORSCHE
STUTTGART

MILD MENTHOL
WEED
Cigarettes

www.ingramcontent.com/pod-product-compliance
Lightning Source LLC
Chambersburg PA
CBHW080605220526
45466CB00010B/3252
* 9 7 8 1 6 5 7 2 9 2 8 4 0 *